FREEDOM

HOW I FOUND FREEDOM IN THE MIDST OF DEPRESSION, ANXIETY, AND PAIN

WILL GUTIERREZ

CONTENTS

PRAISE FOR FREEDOM

This book gives me hope! Pastor Will brings to his obvious talent and passion a rare honesty and vulnerability. As pastors, Jesus calls us to love, which we can't do unless we feel deeply in our hearts. As creatives and musicians, we are divinely designed to experience the extremes of beauty and sorrow. And as leaders called to believe for great and impossible things, things that take miracles, we will know more than our share of anxiety, disappointment, loss and depression. For a young pastor like Will to realize, "Embracing your emotions doesn't mean you don't have faith - we can have hope and faith and still feel all the pain and sorrow life brings," gives this veteran pastor great hope for the next generation of God's leaders. Will took off the mask of performance, and in that vulnerability, found the face of grace. You will too as you read his powerful witness.

Dr. David T. Goh, Senior Pastor at The Garden Bakersfield

Will's passion to help people discover the freedom found in Christ is unreal. He's become a good friend to me and I can attest that he is the real deal! Will is a gifted communicator and his vulnerability and story will not only bring tears to your eyes, but will shine a bright light on the gospel. This is the book of the year!

Zach Maldonado, Bestselling author of *The Cross Worked.* and *Perfect and Forgiven*, pastor at Church Without Religion, and speaker

There is a "dark night of the soul," "an evil day," that comes to each one of us. No matter how prepared we are for it, we must still walk through this "valley of the shadow of death." No person who has greatness in them can avoid going through it no matter how great our faith is. To remain in it is torment; to finally exit it into the light of a new day fills us with hope for a glorious future. Will's testimony that the same truth of God's infinite love that saved you is the same truth that will hold you close and finally set you free is compelling and real. The impact of Will's life is enormous; I've observed it up close since he was in his late teens. His gifting to speak prophetically to people about where they are at and what God sees them as is keenly felt throughout this book. I recommend it!

Dr. Micheal Petzer

Being in a sport like boxing, this book, *Freedom*, has helped me out and gave me the proper wisdom I need to walk out my faith as a man of God in such a lonely, crooked sport. Definitely would recommend all, not just athletes, but all to give it a read.

Miguel Contreras, Professional boxer

I am so grateful that Will has been bold enough to share with us his struggles with hopelessness, depression & thoughts of suicide. In a world that needs hope, Will points us to hope in Jesus in an authentic way. You will leave this book feeling better than you began!

Jon Norman, Senior pastor of Soul Church UK Norwich England

It's raw, it's real, and it's relevant! Will is a voice we so need in the days that we're living. However, the voice you'll hear resonating throughout this book, will not only be his, but that of the Holy Spirit. You'll experience such hope as you are led to a place of discovering that the prison doors you believed shut you out or held you in, have already been unlocked. My personal discovery through this book was that "freedom" is a "kingdom" one that we should all be living in! Freed not only from our past, but freed to live out our God given purpose! This precious, gifted young man, will take you on a wild, and unforgettable journey into the very core of the character of our Father God. Young or old, regardless of position, education or experience, this is a must read. At its center you will find that its purpose will drive us back to the place we all should be living in. That is the life Christ has promised when He said "I have come that you might have life and have it more abundantly." Thank you, my friend, for helping each one of us, "become more, do more, live more, and love more." Your genuine, generous heart will speak for years and years to come.

Pastor Rob Spina

I have known Will Gutierrez for more than a decade. He worked on my staff for six years as a youth pastor, a worship leader and part of the teaching team. He's also my son. He's been married to my daughter Amanda for more than 9 years. In every aspect that I have known Will; as husband, father, leader, and friend, he has always inspired those around him with an abiding love for life, a deep trust in God, and a boundless loyalty to family and friends. I was incredibly blessed by this book, it is a culmination of a lifetime of curiosity. Of asking hard questions and wrestling with the answers. Will's story will inspire and encourage you to continue your journey in Christ, to never quit and never give up.

Ken Spicer, Lead Pastor at Hope Unlimited Church

Freedom by Will Gutierrez is a very honest and to the point read. In it, Gutierrez bravely takes you on his own personal journey through the dark and painful times he experienced into the victory, freedom, and understanding that He found in and through Christ alone. He reveals very clearly the lessons that he gained in these moments and parallels them really well to well know characters in the gospels who walked similar roads. I believe that many people in these days we now find ourselves with all its challenges will be able to relate to the brutally honest stories and accounts contained in it and will also find new strength, hope, and direction from it. I have known Will for many years now and I'm thankful for him being so vulnerable in His writing of this.

Andy Elmes, Lead Pastor of Family Church and founder of Greatbiglife.co.uk

FREEDOM

*How I Found Freedom in the Midst of
Depression, Anxiety, and Pain*

WILL GUTIERREZ

Freedom

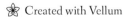

INTRODUCTION

Let me break the ice. I've struggled with depression, I've battled against anxiety, I've overcome the lie of suicidal thoughts, and I've been a victim to abandonment, anger, and loss. I've carried the weights of grief, disappointment, and sorrow. I've been the punching bag of sickness, poverty, and insecurity.

You probably wouldn't believe this if you met me, but with all these issues and insecurities, God thought it would be a great idea to call me to be a pastor. I'm also a husband to a beautiful woman who truly loves Jesus and a father to three handsome boys who have more energy than I can explain. According to the world, I'm not supposed to struggle with depression. People would rather have me be quiet about that battle.

I wrote this book to let you know that you are not alone in your struggle. Whatever the fight may be, God is on your side. You're not weird or unusual for the way you feel. You're not less-than for your battle. My hope is that this book will bring encouragement to you as I open my heart and share my story. Along the way, I pray that you find freedom from many of the lies you're believing and that you can walk in the new identity that God has promised for your life.

CHAPTER 1

LIFE IS WORTH LIVING

As a pastor, I knew how to pray all the prayers. I knew how to worship God and listen to all the music. I knew how to read the Bible. I knew who to seek and who to pray to. I knew how to do all the "spiritual" things I was told to do.

But I was struggling. I was hurting. I was in pain. I was in a drought. It was a devastating and difficult time—no doubt the darkest season of my life. I had just taken a position as the senior pastor of an amazing church. But like any other change in life, there were a lot of new, difficult transitions, not only for me but also for the people of the church. There I was, in my twenties, taking on this new role, and I felt like a lot of people were against me. I felt alone, neglected, and like no one appreciated my leadership style, my youth, or the direction I wanted to take the church.

Little by little, the negativity and judgment I felt began weighing heavily on me. We had moved hours away from our families, so we had no friends and no connections. Then we met a family who loved us well. They supported us and were there for us, and it was a godsend.

Not long afterward, their granddaughter got ill, and within weeks she couldn't walk. The doctors didn't know what to do. As the new pastor, I was believing in a miracle for her. But little did we know, she had a rare brain disease. Her life was slipping away. My faith and hope continued, but she went into a coma. A few days later, she went to be with Jesus.

I did her funeral, and for the first time in my life I questioned God. Why wasn't she healed? Feelings that maybe this was my fault crept in, and then sadness, grief, and depression came over me. Parents are not supposed to bury their children.

One night, I woke up to a piercing thought: "Kill yourself now." No matter what I tried, the thought persisted. Actually, it got worse. A flood of emotions overtook me, followed by what felt like a dense fog inside. It was the absence of peace. It was depression in its purest form. All I could envision was putting a gun to my head and ending my life.

I woke my wife, and we put on worship music and began praying. I spoke truth to myself and read God's Word, renewing my mind and taking every thought captive.

I was on an emotional roller coaster. I was literally dizzy from the movement of events playing in my head, and found myself living out and fighting what I had always spoken against. Anytime I would hear a Christian speak about depression, I would assume they weren't reading God's Word enough, praying enough, or seeking God the right way. I would wonder if something was wrong with them.

"You can't be living for Jesus and have any struggle with the Enemy." That was what I'd always been taught, and now I was up against this crazy giant of depression that was trying to destroy me. *I mean, this attack is not from God; it's from the devil,* I told myself. *Totally from the devil and of the devil!*

Am I really doing this right now? Am I okay? Am I of the devil?

Let me pause right here and say, dealing with depression does *not* mean you are of the devil. Thoughts like this may be an attack from the devil, but you are not of him. You are of and in Christ. It's just that the Enemy tries to rob us of focusing in and living out the fullness of life in Christ.

The next day, while in my car, I began feeling worse than I had during the night. It was the darkest moment of my life. My heart and head were pounding. Sweat dripped down my face. I didn't know why I was so anxious and depressed. There I was, alone and ready to end it all. Everything was fighting against me, and I was doing everything I could to cling to hope. But no Bible verse or encouragement could give me hope.

The lies came: "Will, you're a horrible father. You're a terrible husband. You're not a good enough pastor. You're not making a difference." *Why am I alive?* I asked myself. *Why are things happening the way they are? No one cares about me. My life doesn't matter.*

It felt like the Enemy was in the passenger seat, tempting me to drive off the cliff. He convinced me to go for it, and I gripped the wheel and drove as fast as I could. This was my breaking point—literally the moment of life or death.

Screaming, "Ahhhh, stop!" I slammed on the brakes. Tire smoke surrounded me. I was stuck in the middle of the road, and so was my life. Did I keep going or did I stop?

In that moment I thought, *Am I going to leave my wife without a husband, my kids without a father, my church without a pastor, and my friends without a friend?* I had to make a decision. I blared the car radio with worship music, and as I stepped out of the car, I prayed for God to take away everything I had been struggling with. I rebuked every lie from Satan, yelling, "Get out! Get out! Get the heck out of my car, get out of my head!" I cried my eyes out, weeping and gasping for air. "Please, Lord," I begged. "Help me to hear and see you through all of this."

After reciting every Bible verse I could remember, I felt the Lord wanted me to be silent and just receive what He had for me. And in that moment I started to truly understand the value and love God has for me. And now I'm alive to tell you this story and give you hope and a reason to not give up on life. Instead, give everything to God.

Perhaps you're like me and you've entertained suicidal thoughts. Or maybe it hasn't reached that point, but you constantly struggle with worry, anxiety, negative thinking, fear, or depression. And maybe you're like me and you're wondering, *Is this normal? Is it okay that I think these things? Where are these thoughts coming from? Is there something wrong with me?*

I used to be ashamed when speaking about my struggle. I thought that as a leader, I needed to be strong and have it all together. But what I've realized is that there's power in our testimony.

There are moments in all of our lives that build us up or break us down. This broke me. But what if every situation, negative or positive, can be turned around for good? That's totally a God thing. He wants to turn and work all things out for the good. In situations we think nothing good can come from, God will show us the light.

I received a call from one of my close friends, Traci, who has been a huge part of my life since I was a young music artist traveling the world. The moment I pressed the green button to accept her call, I knew something was wrong. Before I could even put the phone to my ear, I heard weeping and sobbing. If death had a specific sound, that was it.

"Are you okay?" What's wrong?" I asked.

The crying and sobbing continued. Then trying to catch her breath, she yelled, "He's dead!"

"Who? Traci, who is dead?"

"Jared. He killed himself."

Our good friend who we had done close work and ministry with was gone. He was a young man who had a ministry for those struggling with depression—a young man who was a pastor just like me. He had a wife and small children, just like me. He was a bright light for everyone around him. And now just like that, boom. Gone.

In that moment, I sensed God calling me to be a voice to the voiceless. To share the hope of the gospel with those who struggle with depression. The message He wants me to proclaim is: By the power of Christ in you, you can overcome the lie. You don't have to give into Satan's plans. You don't have to buy the lie that you're not enough, the false idea that you are not loved or valuable. It's time to declare freedom over every heart and mind.

I've lost too many people in my life to suicide. And my passion is to help you see the truth of who you are in Christ, see the goodness of God, and see what God is doing the midst of your struggle with depression, anxiety, doubt, confusion, worry, or pain.

In this book, we're going to look at the lies we've believed about depression and then the truth that Jesus promises will set us free. We're going to look at the promises God has for you and me in the midst of our struggle. And then we're going to talk about how to move forward and about God's path of healing.

Here's what I want you to know as truth: God is for you. He's not against you. Life is worth living. There's nothing wrong with you. You're enough in Christ. God is in you and He is with you—forever. Even in the midst of your worst thoughts and worst moments, God is there.

Jesus overcame the lies of Satan. He combated the devil with truth, with the Word of God. And since He lives in you, you can overcome the lies too. To God, you're worth the sacrifice of Jesus. You have more value than you know. Jesus didn't die to shame you but to save you. And so He'll never use shame or guilt to set you free. You're already as close to Jesus as you'll ever be. This isn't a book about you striving to get more of His presence, love, or acceptance.

Since God has qualified you forever, no struggle can disqualify you from God using you. God isn't mad at you. He's crazy in love with you. Your greatest days are ahead because God is never late. His timing is perfect, and since you're in Him, He's got you! God will never quit on you or give up on you. Even if you have absolutely no faith, God remains faithful to you (see 2 Timothy 2:13).

God's grace has you. There's nothing you can do to remove yourself from His presence or His grace. There's nothing you can do or think or feel that will cause Him to love you less. God's love and care for you is based on what Christ has done for you, not what you do or don't do.

God is working everything that has ever happened to you for your good. That's why I believe your greatest days are ahead of you. Your life matters. Your story matters. And I know that God wants to do immeasurably more than we can ever ask or imagine (see Ephesians 3:20)!

CHAPTER 2

VOICELESS

There isn't much that's worse than dealing with an issue in your life that you can't talk to anyone about. You want to open up, but you hesitate to express anything because you fear that it will change people's views about you. So you stay silent. You bury every emotion and don't release anything.

At the beginning of my life, I couldn't speak. I had no voice. Literally, I couldn't talk. When I would open my mouth to speak, people couldn't hear what I was saying. My parents had no idea what was wrong with me. I was always gasping for air too, and finally we figured out that I had a disease. But the doctors couldn't really give us a name or tell us what it was.

At the age of three, I was rushed into emergency surgery because I wasn't able to breathe. That's when they discovered a growth in my airway and my voice box. The doctors said if I didn't have the surgeries to remove them, I could suffocate and die. The only way to remove the growth was laser surgery. Thank God they never had to cut me open. The uncomfortable part was that they had to stick wires down my nose in order to remove the growths.

I always dreaded these surgeries because the doctors told me there was a chance I could die on the operating table. Every time I went to the hospital, I was paralyzed with fear—terrified of what could happen and the physical pain after these operations. For the first two years I had surgery every three weeks, and I hated it each time because I wasn't able to eat for days after each operation. And being so young, I didn't know how to process all of this.

By the time I was five, I had already had over forty surgeries. In my mind, I knew I was different. I wasn't like everyone else. I've always had this struggle and battle for acceptance. Up to that point, I had never really experienced love or care. I felt trapped, alone, and sad. Even as a child, I fought depression. I didn't know my value, and I didn't know that I was loved.

I love my parents. They're some of the most amazing people in this world, and they now pastor a church and are two of my closest friends. But for the first five years of my life, my parents were addicted to drugs. Psychologically, we learn a lot about who we are from the first five years of our life. What I picked up and learned from my early upbringing were addiction, poverty, abuse, turmoil, and self-neglect.

One day, my mom cried out to the Lord and said, "If I hear my son's voice, I'll serve you, I'll go to church, and I'll do whatever you want me to do, Lord." She wasn't in her right mind when she prayed this prayer. She was most likely high.

But days later, I walked into her bedroom and for the first time ever, she heard me whisper, "Mom!"

She jumped up, completely shook, then ran to my dad and said, "Listen to your son! Listen to your son. He's talking. He has a voice. I can't believe it! I just heard him speak!"

"No way!" my dad said.

And right then, I whispered, "Dad, I can talk!" This was a miracle.

What a celebration for them. And this wasn't the end of this victorious story. That same day, their drug dealer came knocking at the front door—not to sell them drugs but to invite them to church. I can't make this up. He began to tell them about his encounter with Jesus.

From my mom's prayer, to hearing my voice, to then being invited to church. Their lives were never the same. They also encountered Jesus. Leaving everything behind, they devoted themselves to Christ from that day forward. And although they had dealt with my illness poorly in the beginning, their transformation in Christ radically changed their care for and relationship with me. From that day forward, my parents were devoted to prayer and believing for my healing.

I was going to school and still struggling with my voice. I was still having surgeries on my throat, and it didn't help that I sounded like The Godfather. I was so embarrassed by my voice, and being bullied and feeling worthless caused me to have anxiety about going to school. I feared talking in front of people, or the teacher calling on me or making me read aloud. I questioned my position in life and doubted God's care for me. I had so much anger toward myself and toward God, and dealt with so many insecurities and self-doubt.

During all of this, there was a woman who randomly came to our house and told my mom that she was led by the Spirit to come and pray for me. My mom trusted that the woman was hearing from God even though we didn't know who she was or what she was about, so she allowed the woman into our home.

The woman placed her hands on my throat, not knowing that was the very place I needed healing. And she then began to speak and prophesy that I would travel the world, preach the gospel, sing, and rap for Jesus.

My mom was furious—because how could this woman speak such words?

Nothing changed for me after that day. Even though there was a word spoken over my life and God wanted my attention, I took a detour. As a teenager, I started hanging out with the wrong people and got involved in gangs and all the worst things people can think about. I was living my life in opposition to the will of God. At my core, I wanted acceptance and love, but I didn't want it from God.

I was unaware of what God wanted for me. I was lost and confused about myself, and being devoured by the sin of my life. I had lost friends to prison and even had some of my closest friends murdered. Then at fifteen, I began dating the girl who lived across the street from me. It was a notebook-type romance. I would walk her to school and home every day.

Everything seemed great until one evening I received a phone call from my mom, who told me I needed to come home immediately. I didn't know what to expect. As I neared my house, I saw the ambulance, the police, the fire department. They had my girlfriend's house taped off. At that moment, I saw a covered body being put into a white van.

The girl I was dating had committed suicide.

My dad tried to offer me comfort and invited me to church. I showed up that next week, and a man I had never met was speaking. He had crazy amounts of energy and passion in his voice. In the middle of his message, he stopped everything he was preaching and pointed right at me and said, "God has a plan for you! Stop running!"

This frustrated me. Why would this man call me out and embarrass me in front of everyone? Angry, I stood up and started walking toward the back door.

At the top of his lungs he shouted, "The devil tried to take your voice away!"

I froze. He didn't know what was wrong with me.

He then said, "You have a voice for the world, and God has called you to travel the world, preach the gospel, sing, and rap for Jesus." He spoke over me the same words that I heard when I was five years old.

Right then, I knew God was real. I felt an overwhelming peace and love that I'd never experienced before. Don't get me wrong, it took me over a year to fully believe in all that God wanted to do with me. I usually went to church just to please my parents, and I would even try to bring my gang-member friends to church with me while still living a double life in gangs but in church. I was torn between two way-different lifestyles.

But it's okay to be in the process. That's why we're told to renew our minds with the truth of God's Word each day. We're not always going to feel loved and valued and accepted. It may take days or months or years for us to stop believing the lies of old and start believing the truth of the new that sets us free.

Maybe you haven't had someone stop a whole service and speak over your life or maybe you've never "heard from God." You might be questioning everything and thinking, *Where is my Jesus moment?* Let me be the first to tell you: You're qualified and equipped to be used by God to change the world. God has a plan for your life. And there's so much that God wants to do in and through your life that is better than anything you could ever ask for or imagine. God loves you and wants to use you in great ways, and He calls you His child. You might not be called to traveling the world, but you're called to greatness and God definitely wants to use you.

Just like me, you cannot thwart or ruin the call God has for you. Romans 11:29 tells us that "the gifts and the calling of God are irrevocable." You have a voice. You have a purpose. You have value. Don't let anyone tell your otherwise. First Peter

2:9–10 tells us that we are part of "a chosen race, a royal priesthood, a holy nation, a people for God's own possession." This means nothing can alter God's opinion of you and nothing can remove you from God's love or presence (see John 10:28; Romans 8:38–39).

God cares deeply for you. And He promises to work out everything—all the ugly parts of your story—for your good (see Romans 8:28). God is not ashamed to call you His child (see Hebrews 2:11; 11:16). He's never going to leave you, no matter how messy life gets (see Hebrews 13:5). Your life is hidden in Christ, which means in every moment you are safe with Him (see Colossians 3:3). Yes, even in the midst of your depression and anxiety, God promises to be with you and for you.

Even though you may not feel this, it's true. God's truth, not your feelings, is what is true about you. You're more than a conqueror (see Romans 8:37). It may feel like your thoughts and circumstances are winning the day, but you can take heart, because Christ has overcome the world (see John 16:33). He gets the final word, not your circumstances. Keep on pushing forward.

When this evangelist spoke those words over me, I wasn't a preacher, I wasn't a singer, and I most definitely wasn't a rapper. Like, I'd never rapped. He told me that he wanted me to perform at a crusade in three months—rapping—and that God would stir up a song in me. So like any teenager, I went home, listened to secular music, and started replacing words with the word *Jesus*.

You may be thinking, *How can God use me? I'm such a mess.* Or *I have no talent.* Here's the good news: God calls us to walk by faith, not sight. He wants us to trust Him, not what we see or what we think is true. This is all the process. God is God of the impossible. I had never rapped, and yet by God's grace, I ended up doing my own song at that crusade. At that same event, I was discovered by radio stations and TV programs, and within eight months I was an official rapper. I was being paid a little over full-time wages to travel and do events, by the time I was eighteen years old.

Your story is probably different. Chances are, it's not rapping that God has called you to, but your story isn't over. Whatever God calls you to, He is faithful to see you through it (see 1 Thessalonians 5:24).

Everyone has a story. And everyone has a voice. It's crazy for me to think back and see that what the Enemy tried to take from me is the very thing God is using from me to change lives. There's power in your voice. The Enemy may try to convince us that we are voiceless—that God and everyone else can't hear us. But the Enemy is a liar, and I believe God wants to use you and your story to give hope to those around you.

The biggest lie our generation believes is that our voice doesn't matter and our voice isn't going to bring that much change to this messed-up world. I might not change the whole world, but I can impact and change someone's world. Maybe you're like me when I was a child. I would try to speak, but no one was listening or no one could hear me. But what if I told you that your voice is being heard, that your story does matter, and that you can and will be a beacon of hope to those around you?

Don't receive the lie that your voice doesn't matter. Your life can and is making an impact. But you're going to need to open your mouth. Get bold, come alive. Walk out the God-given life you've been blessed to have.

For a long time, I've wrestled—even recently—with the question of whether or not I should share my story of depression. Some people don't respond well to those suffering with depression, like in some of the Christian circles I've seen, so I was scared of what others would think of me as a pastor and leader. I didn't realize it was okay to struggle.

I thought I might be disqualified in people's eyes. What I've realized, though, is that people may disqualify me, but I'm always qualified by God because of what Christ has done. Second Corinthians 3:6 says God "has qualified us [making us sufficient] as ministers of a new covenant" (AMP).

We need to stop allowing what people say about us to hinder what God wants to do through us. Nothing should stop us from sharing our story. There's power in your testimony, and your story can set others free. People need to hear what you've been through, whatever it may be—divorce, bankruptcy, loss, prison, addiction, depression, or family problems. Whatever it is that you've experienced in life, God wants to turn it around and use it to bring freedom and hope to others!

Second Peter 1:3 tells us that "His divine power has granted to us all things that pertain to life and godliness." This means you are fully equipped to do all that God is calling you to. You're enough. You have what it takes. Colossians 2:10 says you're complete in Christ. So don't doubt what God wants to do in you and through you. Get ready to impact someone's world. You never know. Your yes to Jesus may eventually impact the whole world.

CHAPTER 3

WHEN WE DOUBT

One night I had a dream that I was standing on a diving board high up in the sky. Pretty random, right? As I looked down into this gigantic pool, the water was calm—absolutely no movement. I was bouncing and balancing myself on this diving board, hesitant to jump because of the height. And then I suddenly jumped. As I made a big splash, I woke up.

I wanted immediate answers.

Looking for a translation to this dream, I prayed, but nothing came. So I opened the Bible and still nothing. Then— boom—I knew where I could get the final answer: Google! (I say that as a joke, but I really did google high diving boards and big pools. The closest pool to my dream was an Olympic-size pool.)

Did you know that an Olympic-size pool holds 660,000 gallons of water? That's crazy insane to me. Did you also know that one gallon equals 8.3 pounds? So, if you do the math, 660,000 gallons x 8 = 5,280,000 pounds. I didn't even add the

0.3 in there for the sake of keeping my sanity. But that totals over 5 million pounds of water. That's ridiculous.

How does this tie into this chapter? Well, let me share what's special about this dream and what God revealed to me through it:

1. It took me back to my childhood and a special moment with my best friend.
2. It revealed to me our true potential as sons and daughters of God.

I jumped off of the diving board, and as soon as I landed in the calm water, there was movement. Not only was there a splash but also a shift in the whole body of water. You can try this in any pool. As soon as you jump in, there's a shift. You can see the ripple effect and the movement of the water even after you get out.

Regardless of your height or weight in the physical, you can make an impact in the spiritual. You are tiny compared to 5,280,000 pounds, but no matter how small you think you are, you can cause movement. God is calling us out of comfort and into a life of fullness with Him. You have to take the leap of faith. Jump into your calling and purpose.

When you decide to jump, it will cause a shift and movement. But so many times we decide to keep it safe and not take the leap because we are in doubt. I've been there. I've doubted my purpose, my calling, my identity, my value, and my worth, and I've doubted God. Doubt is one of the biggest hindrances for us as children of God.

When we doubt what we are qualified to do, we put God's promises into question. One thing I've learned throughout my short thirty-two years of life is that God always comes through and always wants what's best for me even when I question Him or doubt myself.

My life is filled with crazy experiences, a lot of which I wish I had never gone through. What I realize is that every experience created strength. At six years old, I finally had a voice but it was more of a whisper. Even so, I was known as the wild child. I've been told my whole life that I need to relax and take a chill pill because my energy level is way above sea level.

One day I was at my babysitter's house. Her name was Gloria, and she was always happy and full of joy, so I loved being around her. But just like any house I went to for child care, there were rules. I couldn't go in the backyard because there was a pool there. And I couldn't go in the front yard because there were cars there. Of course, I did the opposite of what Gloria told me.

One day, I heard some music and playful shouting along with sounds of water splashing, so I went to the backyard, where I was hearing it from. I saw the pool, but I couldn't swim so of course I wasn't going to jump in. I looked up, and there he was on the diving board—bouncing up and down, ready to jump in.

I realized the boy had a deformity. His upper body was normal but his legs were very short. His hands almost touched the ground. As I was staring at him, he looked at me. With my raspy, froggy voice, I asked, "Why are your legs like that?"

He responded, "Why is your voice like that?"

I froze. Taken back and slightly offended, I finally said, "I was born this way."

He grinned. "Me too."

Joseph Garcia became my best friend.

Here's the thing about Joseph. He could do anything and everything other kids could do, but better. He was laser focused on everything he set his heart on. He was the best wrestler and swimmer I had ever met. He even taught me how to swim. He could breakdance, skateboard, and do pretty much anything that everyone else said was impossible. He had no limitations.

Why do we put limits on God? And why do we allow limitations to hold us back? We have so many excuses. We say, "I was born this way," or "My mom and dad were that way," or "It's been in the family forever." I'm fat. I'm stupid. I'm angry. I'm no good. Have you caught yourself saying something like this? We take on these false identities and allow them to limit us from being the full sons and daughters that God has called us to be.

We think there are limitations to what God wants to do in our life. We allow all these limitations—past sins, physical traits, scars, opinions—to stop us from living out our true freedom in Christ. But I want to destroy every lie that you've believed. You've been born again, and you literally have Jesus Christ living in you (see Galatians 2:20).

First John 4:4 tells us that "greater is He who is in you than he who is in the world." Do you recognize that you are united to Christ (see Romans 6:5)? That you have been joined to Jesus (see 1 Corinthians 6:17)? This means you have access to the God of the universe 24/7. When the thoughts and accusations come, you can look to Jesus knowing He is for you and not against you (see Romans 8:31).

And when you doubt what He says about you, remember this: "If we are faithless, He remains faithful" (2 Timothy 2:13). All the promises of God find their *yes* in Christ (see 2 Corinthians 1:20). Do you realize that God's promises to you are based on what Christ has done, not on what you do? God promises to meet all your needs (see Philippians 4:19). He promises to never forsake you (see Hebrews 13:5). He promises to guard your heart and mind (see Philippians 4:7). These and so many more!

You are the righteousness of God in Christ (see 2 Corinthians 5:21). This means that you are a partaker of the divine nature (see 2 Peter 1:4) and that you are fully equipped and qualified to live righteous and holy. God says you've been made righteous because of Jesus's obedience for you, not your obedience for Him (see Romans 5:19). This means we are not obeying in order to become righteous; we obey because we are righteous. Since we are accepted by Christ, we live our lives rooted and grounded in His unconditional acceptance of us (see Romans 15:7).

Since you're in Christ, you're dead to sin (see Romans 6:11). This means that every negative thought that comes your way has no power or authority over you since you're under God's grace (see Romans 6:14). You have the mind of Christ (see 1 Corinthians 2:16). This enables you to choose God's thoughts even in the midst of the lies and accusations that come at you.

We can use the excuse that we were born a certain way, but no matter how you were born physically, you've been born again—spiritually. You can no longer use the past as a reason to not live a life of fullness and passion now. There are no limitations to who you are as a new creation, and what Christ can do in and through your life.

Joseph Garcia taught me a lot, and I can honestly say I don't know where I would be without his impact in my life. He was actually the person who got me involved in hip-hop. Yup! My best friend was the legit rapper. I just followed in his footsteps. It was a long process because of the detours and roads I decided to take in life, but I eventually started traveling with my best friend doing hip-hop concerts and youth conferences, camps, and crazy venues with thousands of sold-out believers.

I could write an entire book on how we traveled the world and how many lives Joseph and I partnered up with Christ to impact. You have to partner and surround yourself with good friends who are "God friends"—people who want the best for you and aren't afraid to straighten you out at times. I'm blessed to say Joseph Garcia is family to me, and I believe we all need someone like him in our lives.

Who are you surrounding yourself with? Are you only around people who are speaking negatively over you? People who bring you down and who are not allowing you to live the abundant life Christ has given you? The Bible says, "Two are better than one ... for if either of them falls, the one will lift up his companion" (Ecclesiastes 4:9–10).

The greatest thing about connecting with others is it gives you an opportunity to encourage them and for them to encourage you. Iron sharpens iron. The crazy thing about sharpening iron is sometimes sparks fly. Friendship won't always be easy, but it will always be worth it. We all need someone in our lives to keep us accountable and lift us up when we need it.

Do you have people around you who will pray for and encourage you and speak truth to you? The people around you can produce good or bad things in your life and in your mind. It is so important that you surround yourself with good people who will walk with you in all seasons, good and bad.

Joseph and I both had our insecurities. We both learned how to build around all the negativity we received. We did everything together. Our music started to gain traction and we were traveling a lot, and in 2006 I introduced him to a girl who would eventually become his wife. Fast-forward to 2011, when I got married, and he was part of my wedding. If it wasn't for my having a blood brother, Joseph would have been my best man. He said, "Don't trip, Will. I know I'm really the best man, but I'll stand next to your brother."

Joseph was always cracking crazy jokes and pranks, so I never knew what was going to be real or not. Everything was a surprise. One day he called and told me he had just been diagnosed with leukemia. That ended up being totally true. So we did what any Holy-Ghost-believing Christian would do: we rebuked it and started praying for healing. Blessed to say that one year later, he was cancer-free. Thank you, Jesus! We celebrated greatly for this miracle. I believe in healing and miracles because I believe that's who our God is—a healer, a restorer, a miracle worker.

This became a vital part of Joseph's story. When speaking, we would start out our events by saying, "Joseph couldn't walk. And I couldn't talk. And the devil tried to give him cancer, but now he's cancer-free. I've had all these throat surgeries and doctors said I would never speak, and now I'm disease-free." We would pump up the crowd by reminding them of the God we serve who heals and sets us free.

Eventually, I decided it would be best to slow down all the travels and become more present with my family. I took a job as an assistant pastor at an awesome church in Southern California. I was preaching one morning, and after the third service I remember picking up my phone to look at my fantasy football scores (because you know that's what every pastor should be focused on—it was Sunday after all). I had one more service to go, but I realized I had seven missed calls from Joseph. So I did what any good friend would do: I called him back and said, "What the heck do you want, bro? I'm married and you're blowing up my phone."

Joseph responded in a soft, relaxed voice, "Hey, what's up lubbyG?" That was his nickname for me. He proceeded to tell me that I needed to get to the hospital as soon as possible because the cancer was back.

I responded, "The devil is a liar and rebuke that lie. Walk by faith, my brotha. We've seen it disappear once and Jesus will do it again!"

But he said, "No, Will. You don't understand." He broke down crying, and that's when I knew it was serious. "The doctors say I only have seventy-two hours to live."

I stopped what I was doing and drove straight to the hospital.

We prayed and worshipped for hours that night. We were believing God for another healing. At 3:34 a.m., when I told Joseph to go to sleep because all of his friends and family would be visiting that morning, we prayed our last prayer and believed God that Joseph would receive his miracle. I hugged him, told him I loved him, and fell asleep at his left hand, his wife at his right hand. We woke up a few hours later but Joseph never did; his miracle was entering into the gates of heaven.

I didn't know that was going to be the last time I talked to my best friend. I didn't know that I was going to be the last person to ever speak to him. That was the beginning of the whirlwind of deep sadness, depression, and everything that comes with loss.

As a pastor, I was well acquainted with loss. But something was different about this one. It hit harder than anything I'd ever experienced. I can't express the weight of grief I was carrying. That night I was forced to jump straight into "pastor mode" with his family. Instead of grieving, I was giving counsel to everyone else and planning the funeral with his family. And all I could think about was how I was going to do my best friends funeral and what I needed to say and the order of events for the service. Looking back now, I realize why I slid into such a deep depression for a few months after He went to be with the Lord.

Maybe you've been through loss. In that season, there's sadness and sorrow, pain you can't explain. And as we know, there's a time for everything. A time to weep and a time to mourn. But there's also a time to dance and rejoice (see Ecclesiastes 3:1–8). Maybe you've been there, through those seasons of hopelessness, and are wondering why this happens. We don't have all the answers, but we don't need to create a theology to answer why some die and why some live. We need to know that God is good and that He is for us, not against us. That He is a healer. That He gives hope. That He gives life.

It's okay to weep. It's okay to be sad. It's okay to have emotions and to feel depressed. Maybe, even now, you need to pause, take a deep breath, and say, "I'm okay." Or "I'm allowed to feel sad." You need to realize that this is normal. Sometimes we go through emotional days not even knowing why we feel the way we feel. Just know that God wants to hold you and He wants you to trust Him with your heart.

Jesus knew all about healing. He walked in it and performed it. He knew the outcomes His hands would have. His friend Lazarus was dead, and we all know the Scripture that says, "Jesus wept" (John 11:35). He felt the pain and sorrow of His friend's death. Jesus, God Himself, felt what we felt. He embraced his emotions. So don't try to brush your feelings under the rug. It's okay to feel pain and sadness.

There's a lie that "If you have more faith, then bad things won't happen. If you are really seeking Jesus, you won't feel pain or sadness." But that's not true. Embracing your emotions doesn't mean you don't have faith. We can have hope and faith and still feel all the pain and sorrow life brings. Jesus knew Lazarus would rise again and He still wept. And in the same way, we know Christ is coming back and will make all things new and yet we are allowed to weep.

God is calling you to take a leap of faith into this season

with full confidence in who He is, but the only way to jump into fullness of life is to truly trust God and move all doubt to the side. That doesn't mean questions or concerns won't rise up in moments of difficulty. It just means we have greater confidence, knowing who's hands we are in.

We might not have the process all down pat and perfect, but we can always trust the one who is perfect—Jesus.

CHAPTER 4

LIGHT IN DARKNESS

In moments of hardship, loss, or grief, we're usually not seeing clearly. Most of the time we're in complete darkness. When walking in or through these seasons of pain, you may feel as if you're lost and have no direction or desire for what's next. Hope seems to vanish in the darkness.

One night when I was ten years old and hanging out with my cousins, it was getting late, so they decided to take me home. It was dark outside, and no one was at my house when they dropped me off. All the lights were off and everything was pitch black. I unlocked the front door, and at seeing the dark hallway, chills crawled up the back of my neck. I ran as fast as I could down the hall to turn on the bathroom light, then ran into the kitchen and turned on the light in there. Going room to room, I made sure every light was turned on so I wouldn't be in the dark. I had some ultra-speed that night. I refused to stay in darkness.

What's crazy is I feel like I do the complete opposite in my personal life. A lot of times I just stand there, or I move so slow, soaking in darkness instead of seeking the light. In those moments of darkness, my depression seems to grow and my value seems to diminish. Death seems like the best option. My mind turns as dark as my problems.

This has been the biggest lie from the devil. We don't have to stay in darkness. We have access to light, to God, every single moment of every day. Christ is *inside* you and me.

You might feel like you're walking aimlessly, wanting breakthrough but never truly arriving at that moment of peace. Maybe you have become stagnant with the unknown. You might be at a complete standstill. I've had many seasons of stagnancy, feeling like I'm going but not really moving. Whether it was Joseph passing to cancer, my girlfriend committing suicide, or the loss of other people in my life, in those seasons I felt like I couldn't move and had no hope. I was trapped in darkness. I would ask, *How do I discover the light? How do I get freedom? Where is hope in the midst of tragedy? If I'm not careful and aware of what darkness does, I'll begin walking in its power over me, not even realizing my heart and mind is being devoured.*

Darkness causes sadness and pain. If we stay in that mindset and allow ourselves to continue in it, we can become silent, hopeless, distracted, angry, upset, depressed, and confused. We can feel like life isn't worth living. There have been times when I'd lock myself in my room for multiple days and nights, not wanting to speak to anyone—including my own wife and children. One time it lasted eight days. I didn't want to be around anyone.

After Joseph died, I slipped into deep sadness. I was surrounded by complete darkness. My wife came into my room one day, wondering when I would rebound and bounce back. She reminded me that she needed me, my friends needed me, and my church needed me. And I didn't know what to tell her or what to do. I felt empty.

Maybe you can relate. Maybe you've experienced the

moments of devastation and turmoil and have walked through those painful times. I share this because I want you to realize that even in your darkest days, God wants to give you clear sight. He wants to bring you out of darkness or blindness, and your only hope is Jesus.

I'm reminded of the blind man in Mark 10:46–52 who cried out to Jesus for a miracle. The people around this blind man told him to be silent, but he'd had enough of living in darkness. He wanted to see. He wanted vision, and he wasn't going to allow the people around him to stop his breakthrough. So he screamed and shouted even louder, "Son of David, have mercy on me!"

When Jesus heard this man he went to him and told him his faith had healed him, and immediately he regained his sight. When walking in blindness, you aren't able to see anything but you have an opportunity to believe what you hear. We all have to be cautious about which voices we will allow in our life. Who will you listen to? And who will you believe?

Some will tell you to be silent about your struggle. They will say don't talk about it. But if you really want to be made well, maybe it's time to open up your spiritual mouth, which I believe is your heart, and say "Jesus, you can have it all. Open my eyes so I can see!"

As I think back, I realize that in these seasons of darkness I had no vision but I still had my ears to listen and hear. My wife began to speak hope back into me. Leaders around me started speaking destiny over me. It's in those times of despair and faithlessness that God becomes our strength, our hope, our everything. I love what Jesus tells Paul in 2 Corinthians 12:9: "And He has said to me, 'My grace is sufficient for you, for power is perfected in weakness.'"

God doesn't shame us for being weak and needy. Actually that's right where he wants us to be, so we can be open and vulnerable. It's in those moments of despair that we trust and depend on Him in a different way.

Paul goes on to say in verse 9, "Most gladly, therefore, I will rather boast about my weaknesses, so that the power of Christ may dwell in me." Instead of being ashamed of what he's going through, Paul brags about his weakness because he knows God's power is in Him—and that by God's power, he is an over-comer. By God's power, you are too.

There have been many moments in my life when I didn't tap into the reality of God's power in me. It's usually because I'm focused on the problem more than the person of Christ. I'm focused more on my weakness than the power of Christ. And when I'm so focused on the problem, I usually feel trapped and think there's no way out.

Obviously, depression and sadness creeps in and that becomes my reality. Fear becomes my reality. I long for freedom but have no ability to move because I'm afraid. And it's as if I'm ten years old again standing in the pitch-black hallway all alone but needing to make a decision. Do I stand here in complete darkness and allow my mind to play tricks on me? Or do I go to the source of light?

The switch! JESUS!

We all can turn on the switch. Life might seem dark and horrible, but the reality is that Christ is in us and we are in light and we are in the kingdom of God's beloved Son (see Colossians 1:13). God's Word tells us this: "For you are all sons of light and sons of day. We are not of night nor of dark-ness" (1 Thessalonians 5:5). And Ephesians 5:8 says that we are "light in the Lord" and that we can "walk as children of Light."

You're not in darkness. Life may look dark and seem dark, but you are in light. You are in Christ.

Where are you today? What things are you facing or going

through? What losses and pains are you overcoming? What situations are trying to bring you down?

God is telling you to turn on the switch. Set your mind on things above (Colossians 3:2). Set your gaze upon Jesus (see Hebrews 12:2). Recognize who you are in Christ and who has you. You're safe in the Father's hand (see John 10:29). You're sealed by the Spirit (see Ephesians 1:13). And you're hidden in the Son (see Colossians 3:3). Do you recognize how secure you are?

Imagine if I would have gone into my house, walked slowly, and allowed it to stay dark. I would have become more worried and fearful. I would have built more lies on what could happen. A monster, a person, or whatever narrative I could have created in the darkness. In darkness, things that aren't true start to be created.

You may feel depressed, you may feel unworthy, you may feel unloved, and you may feel like you don't matter. None of that is true! You are not what you feel. You are who God says you are. You are not depressed, you are not unworthy, you are not unloved, and you do matter! You are cared for by God. You were bought at a price. You have a new identity. Don't stay in darkness.

Turn on the switch.

This means to think on Jesus. Like Philippians 4:8 tells us, we are to think on things that are true and honorable and just and pure and lovely and commendable and excellent and worthy of praise. And as Peter tells us in 1 Peter 1:13, we are to set our hope fully on the grace of God. It's God's grace that not only saves us but sustains us and strengthens us each and every day.

The thing about darkness is that it is a trip to your mind. As I said, so many things are "created" in the darkness. We so easily get tricked. We think every shadow is something. But when the light is on, the darkness is exposed and every trick is removed. In the darkness, rodents, bugs, and every nasty thing come out, but when the light comes on, they scatter. The Enemy does the same. He loves the darkness. He loves to trick us in the darkness because our vision is not enhanced and we can't see. And it's easier for the Enemy to trick us. But when we flip the switch, we can see the truth over the lies.

The darkness brings in the worst possibilities. The light brings in the best opportunities. When you can clearly see who you are and who Christ is, then you can walk in confidence. There's no true confidence in darkness. When we recognize our unity with Christ, we can walk confidently knowing that greater is He who is in us than he who is in the world. The Enemy cannot touch you (see 1 John 5:18). You're more than a conqueror in Christ (see Romans 8:37)!

God is the Father of lights, not the father of darkness (see James 1:17). His desire is to give you good things and to be for you. He's called you out of darkness and into His marvelous light (see 1 Peter 2:9). And by His grace, He wants to expose the dark lies you have believed about yourself so you can walk in the confidence that is yours as a child of God.

The lie of darkness is not the truth. That's why when I was going through that dark season after Joseph passed away, the only thing that could get me out of that pit was the switch being turned on. And I'm grateful and blessed that there were people around me who encouraged me to turn the light on.

I felt like the paralyzed man in the Bible, hoping and wishing that one day I could get up and walk. But sometimes the switch seems impossible to get to. It seems too far away. The light seems too far away. And so often it feels like we can't move or get up, but God places people in our lives who get up for us and flip the switch even when we can't. And that's when everything turns around.

Who is around you? Who is speaking into your life? Who is carrying you? Who are you allowing in your life, and are they willing to lift you up and carry you when you need them? Are they willing to carry you to the rooftop, rip the tiles off, and place you at the feet of Jesus? We need community, and we need friends who care for our souls.

In that season of darkness, people were speaking life into me even when I couldn't speak it to myself. I was laid out in my bed every day, feeling like I had no way up. Darkness became my new normal. But thank God for my wife and those around me who chose to lift me up and walk me to the light switch. I was the paralyzed man, laid out with no hope, wanting to be made whole but feeling no power in my body. My mind wanted to be there, but my body wouldn't follow.

You're not meant to live this life alone. There are people all around you whom God wants to use to help build you up and encourage you. It's time to step out of darkness and walk in the light. Turn on the switch of fullness of life.

CHAPTER 5

WHAT LIFE IS SUPPOSED TO LOOK LIKE

When I think about freedom, the first person who comes to my mind is Mel Gibson acting as William Wallace in the movie *Braveheart*. The legendary warrior wearing the man-skirt with his shirt halfway hanging off the chest, screaming, "Freedom!" I see myself standing in the grocery store screaming, "Freedom!" Standing on the roof shouting, "Freedom!" In the middle of the highway, or on top of the mountain, yelling, "Freedom!"

Life is supposed to be free, exciting, and full of fun. And when I think about it, the real me, Will, is free! I am exciting. And I'm most definitely full of fun. I'm also passionate about life. I love to travel, joke, hang out with people, play games, dance, and be crazy. People always talk about how much energy I have and ask me why I have a smile on my face all the time.

The real me is always passionate, hyper, and playful. When I'm not allowing the situations or struggles I'm facing to beat me up, I'm actually a really fun person to be around. The life of freedom is the life that God intended for me to live.

That's how God wants you to live too.

Second Corinthians 3:17 tells us that where the Spirit of the Lord is, there is freedom. And since you have the Spirit, you have freedom. That means that every place you walk into, you are carrying freedom and peace with you.

Did you know that it is for freedom that Christ set you free (see Galatians 5:1)? And whom the Son sets free is free indeed (John 8:36). You are free! And God's goal is to convince you of how free you actually are. You've got freedom ready to burst out of you. And what freedom does is it places you in a position that reveals your true identity. Your position is in Him. Your identity is in Him. Nothing else needs to have a voice in your life except Christ and Him crucified.

You're a new creation in Christ Jesus (see 2 Corinthians 5:17). The old has passed away; behold, the new is here! When you live in that reality and that understanding, the lies that come against you won't be able to stand. They are not truth. They are not absolutes. So living in freedom gives you the opportunity to stand righteous and whole as you live in the firm reality that you are a new creation.

God's Word tells us that nothing can separate us from God's love. That we are perfected (see Hebrews 10:14). That we are holy (see Hebrews 10:10). That we have right standing with God (see Romans 5:1). We've been justified (see Romans 3:24). And that there's nothing wrong with you and everything is right with you (see 2 Corinthians 5:21).

Freedom exposes every lie and reveals truth that sets you free. There is no depression or anxiety or condemnation for those in Christ (see Romans 8:1). So every lie that might be thrown your way that will make you think or believe that you are anything but free is a lie. You are whole in Christ Jesus.

I'm not saying that you can't struggle with doubt, anger, depression, or anxiety. What I'm saying is that in Christ you are not what you struggle with. You are not defined or held captive by your thoughts or feelings or worst days. God has set you free.

The distraction comes when loss or trials hit. Like when someone says something negative to me or posts something on social media about me or comments something on my post against me. That can shift my focus, my day, and my mindset. I don't know why I allow people to have this much power over my mind, but I do. And it happens. I have to stop, take a deep breath, and get back to the basics of the gospel and renew my mind.

I know you've been there. You see someone you're close to or desire to be around more write something or post a Facebook or Instagram picture with another friend—without you! You get so frustrated and annoyed because you're not included. Or someone says something you disagree with on social media and the next thing you know you're in a keyboard fight. And then your emotions change and your mind begins to shift. You go from that person who is living free to a person who is an imprisoned, negative ball of energy.

We don't have to allow situations in our life to become our realities. We don't have to allow them to rob our life to the fullest. Don't get me wrong. I'm preaching to myself because I've been there, done that. I've got the T-shirt and the hat that goes with it. I even got custom shoes that I wear. It's not easy. Things happen. Things are said. Situations happen that are beyond our control. People come against us. Things die out. People die. Emergencies happen, and they distort and change our view on life and our day gets ruined.

But this still is not the reality. All of these things can go wrong around us, but that doesn't change who Jesus is in us. No matter what happens around you, it doesn't change the fact that God dwells on the inside of you. Don't get so focused on what's happening around you. COVID, the elections, rumors of war, protests, fights around you, trials with friends and family, the diagnosis from the doctor, the divorce you or someone you know is going through, the friends and family who are leaving or moving, the new job or the old job, the money you used to make, the loss of someone dear, the difficult season, the hardship, the pain, or anything that tries to rise up against you, doesn't stand a chance with the reality of who lives in you.

My son Ezra is very light-skinned and has blue eyes. If I sent you (who have never seen a picture of him) to pick him up from school for me, with no details of his features, you would probably never pick him as my son. And Ezra wouldn't give a second glance at you because he has no relationship with you. But I can promise you this: if I drove to his school and hopped out of my minivan, that little light-skinned, blue-eyed boy would come running to me full speed, screaming, "Daddy"! He knows I'm his.

Do you know you're God's?

Nothing can change the identity you have in Christ. You are a child of God, and there is amazing freedom in Christ Jesus. So let's continue shouting and praising and walking in victory. "Freedom!" is our new mantra.

Even if you can't see it right now, there's power and life in your tongue. I want you to speak hope and proclaim God's truth, saying God is good in the midst of everything you go through. Situations around you may be bad, but God is good. He is faithful, and He will get you through. You can overcome. You can do all things through Christ who strengthens you (see Philippians 4:13). You've been empowered to run and walk forward. Keep running the race.

Hebrews 12:1–2 tells us to lay aside anything that weighs us down. There are weights that we hold onto that God doesn't want us to carry. He wants to be the one who bears our weights and who carries us. Remember, when Mary went to the tomb and it was empty, she went and told John and Peter that Christ's body wasn't there. John and Peter ran to the grave, and the Bible says that John beat Peter to the tomb. I believe Peter didn't make it to the tomb as quick as John did because he was running with a lot of weight. A lot of shame, guilt, and condemnation. You can't run fast when you're holding onto shame.

Just three days before the empty tomb, Peter denied Jesus. He actually disowned Him completely. People asked him if he was one of the disciples and if he followed Jesus, and he denied it all. And now three days after the crucifixion, Jesus's body was gone. Peter was running with a lot of shame and guilt, and there was tremendous weight on his shoulders as he wondered if what Jesus had said about His resurrection was true. Perhaps Peter wondered, *Is Jesus going to deny me now the way I denied Him?* He was probably scared that Jesus would hate him or neglect him or disown him. Peter was running with these weights that didn't need to be there.

Cast your cares upon Christ. He cares for you (1 Peter 5:7). Don't run with shame. Lay aside those thoughts, those distractions, and give it all to Jesus. He is the one who wants to give you a hope and a future. He gives you the freedom. Don't walk in shame, fear, or condemnation. He's not shaming you. Christ is saying, "Shame off of you!"

Jesus endured the shame of your sin at the cross so you wouldn't have to. Shame and guilt were carried for you at the cross, so they're not yours to carry. You are clothed with Christ, not shame. You are standing in grace, not guilt. You are seated with Christ, not your past mistakes. Sin is no longer your master because you are under the power of God's grace (see Romans 6:14).

This is God's promise to you: "For I am confident of this

very thing, that He who began a good work in you will perfect it until the day of Christ Jesus" (Philippians 1:6). Do you see that? God will finish what He started in you. God will carry you through. God will work everything for your good (see Romans 8:28). It's God's work from start to finish.

Paul tells us this in Philippians 2:13: "For it is God who is at work in you, both to will and to work for His good pleasure." Jude 24 says, "Now to Him who is able to keep you from stumbling, and to make you stand in the presence of His glory blameless with great joy." God is the one who holds you up and makes you stand. God is the one who keeps you from stumbling. And God is the one who presents you blameless. You're blameless and forgiven because of what Christ has done, not because of what you do (see Colossians 2:13–14).

Jesus is not ashamed to call you brother or sister (see Hebrews 2:11). Do you realize that you're the pleasing aroma of Christ (see 2 Corinthians 2:15). That you are God's child? I have three beautiful sons, and they are my beloved kids. There's nothing they can do to make me love them less. There's nothing they can do to cause me to leave them. I'm so proud of them and in love with them. How much more does God the Father think of you?

Consider this: I know sin very well—yet my love is deep for my children. Imagine the Love that knew no sin. The love of God that is perfect and sinless. Imagine His love for us. That's perfect love. My human, sin-knowing love for my children is crazy huge, and yet there's a greater love than anything we have ever experienced or given to anyone, and it's the love of God toward us.

Remember the woman caught in adultery? Like with her, while everyone else is wanting to throw stones your way, Jesus is protecting you. Even in the worst moments you face, God is for you. Jesus doesn't want to condemn you. He is kneeling down to your level, loving you right where you're at. God meets you right where you are and reminds you that Jesus isn't condemning you or punishing you. Your depression and anxiety is not punishment from God and is not from God at all.

He isn't breaking us down or shaming us. Instead, He is reminding us to get up and walk, and sin no more. Don't keep shaming yourself. Shame yourself no more. Hate yourself no more. Despise yourself no more.

Walk in freedom now. Walk in wholeness. Walk in the finished work. Be whole. Be free!

CHAPTER 6

GOOD NEWS, NOT GOOD ADVICE

The gospel is good news, not good advice. The gospel is not only what saves us, but what fuels our entire life. The gospel is not just the appetizer, but the entire meal. This is why we need to hear the gospel every single day.

You are complete (see Colossians 2:10). You have been restored (see 2 Corinthians 5:18). The good news is that everything Jesus did and accomplished with His life, death, burial, and resurrection, you have accomplished also. Put simply, when Jesus lived perfectly, it's as if you lived perfectly. When Jesus died, you died with Him. When he took those nails, so did you. You were crucified with Christ (see Galatians 2:20).

When He said, "It is finished," the work was finished for you also. I know, this seems unreal. It doesn't make sense. But that's the good news. All the punishment you deserved, Jesus took on your behalf for you and as you—so you wouldn't have to! There's no punishment left (see Romans 8:1). He took the keys to death and then overcame the grave. And it's as if you did the same. You're an overcomer now, and death has no power over you.

The things we couldn't do in our strength or power, Jesus did for us. Now we can live a holy, redeemed, transformed life because of what Christ has done for us. It's the best news ever!

You are whole. You're lacking no good thing. If you look at Jesus and you think, *Man, how amazing and beautiful and wonderful and mighty He is,* all those things you see, you carry. Christ has given them to you. No, we're not Jesus. That's not what I'm saying. But 1 John 4:17 says, "As He is, so also are we in this world." This means that the same love and favor and beauty that Jesus has, we have.

Depression is no longer your master. Sadness is no longer your master. Shame is no longer your master. Satan is no longer your master. In Christ, you are the master. You are the boss. You hold authority over depression. You hold authority over sadness, pain, grief, sin, and death. You hold power because the power of Christ is in you.

You are not your mistakes. You are not your past. You are not your worst moment. You are not the sins you've committed. You are everything Christ has done. You are transformed and have a new identity. You've been restored to fullness. You are not missing anything. You have everything you need for life and godliness (see 2 Peter 1:3). All because of what Christ has done for you.

In Genesis 35, Jacob was given the name Israel. He had gone through everything from wrestling with the angel of the Lord, to renaming Luz to Bethel, to selling his brother a bowl of beans for a birthright, to marrying Rachel and working over fourteen years to do that, to losing his wife and renaming his son. As he was on his death bed, losing his sight, his son Joseph brought his grandsons Manasseh and Ephrem so Jacob would bless them.

We know that when a father or grandfather blesses their children or grandchildren, it's always a blessing from the right hand. So Joseph placed the older son at his right hand and the younger at his left. Jacob was supposed to bless the firstborn son with the right hand of blessing; this was the greater blessing, and the firstborn was supposed to get the better blessing.

But Jacob crossed his arms. He placed his right hand on the younger son's head. He switched it and gave the younger son the blessing the older son deserved. Here in this story, we see the gospel. We see what happened to us.

God crossed his arms. Jesus deserved everything, but God gave us everything we didn't deserve. Everything Jesus deserved, God gave to us. God gave us the complete blessing. Jesus deserved life but died the death. We deserved death but were given life. You may feel like you were born wrong or like you don't deserve it. But grace...

That's the beauty and wonder of God's grace. Our salvation, our position, our authority, and God's favor for us is because of grace and nothing else. We couldn't work for it or earn it. It was given freely—and God doesn't want us to try to pay it back. Nor is He telling us we owe Him. Instead, He wants us to live from it. To enjoy it. And to simply give thanks for all that's been accomplished. Ephesians 1:3 says we've been blessed with every spiritual blessing in Christ. We lack nothing. *You* lack nothing.

It's so easy to feel like we lack everything because we did nothing. But Christ did everything so we need nothing. I know it's a hard concept. Not because it's hard to explain or hard to understand, but because as humans we feel undeserving and want to talk our way out of inheritance from our heavenly Father. We say things like, "I'm unworthy, I don't deserve to be loved. Why would God give someone like me a second chance? I'm just a wretched man. I'm the biggest sinner ever."

Blah, blah, blah.

There's a story in the Bible where David comes back from battle with his six hundred men, and they return to their home city called Ziklag (1 Samuel 30). When they arrive, all of their homes are burned to the ground. All that remains are ashes. They discover that their city had been raided by the Amalekite army and their wives and children taken as prisoners.

David and his men were exhausted, but they have no time to rest. All six hundred of the men started to turn against David because he was supposed to be the leader and now they wanted to stone him to death. But David encouraged and strengthened himself in the Lord. He told the men that he heard from God and that they were supposed to cross the brook and fight the Amalekites in the enemy territory. All the men got rallied up and followed David. But as they reached the brook, two hundred of the men decided they were too exhausted to cross over and fight. David ended up crossing over with four hundred men, and they ended up defeating the Amalekite army and recovering everything that was stolen from them.

Now this story is already amazing as it is. It doesn't need anything added to it. It's a story of battle, victory, and success. Everything that was lost was recovered. Families were reunited. It's already the best ending a story can have. But there's more to the story.

David and his men who were left alive marched back to the brook where they left the two hundred men behind. Yes, there were some negative words exchanged. David's men we're upset that not everyone was willing to cross over and fight. They felt like the two hundred men who stayed behind didn't deserve anything but to die. They thought, *Let's just kill them right here right now, or maybe we should send them walking with nothing.*

But David said, "No. These two hundred men who stayed behind are just as important as the men who went and fought.

They will get everything that belongs to them—their wives, children, and even the silver and gold that we recovered. They will get everything we fought for and won."

Maybe you know where I'm going with this. It's another story of God's amazing grace. Sometimes we decide we are too tired, too exhausted, too weighed down by the things of this world. Most of us have felt like we can't fight anymore—that there's no possible way we can get up and cross the brook. We decide to lay down and give up.

Days, weeks, and maybe even months pass by. And here comes Jesus saying, "Hey! Remember me? Well, I still remember you. And even when you couldn't go and fight these battles, I crossed over and defeated the Enemy for you. I defeated death for you. I defeated depression for you. I defeated anxiety, anger, lust, pride, jealousy, debt, guilt, shame, sickness, and pain for you."

Everything that you couldn't do in your own strength, Jesus did for you. You're just as important as Jesus who went to battle. You didn't do it, but you get the benefit as if you did because you are in Christ and Christ is in you.

This is the good news. This is the gospel. You don't need to accomplish what's already been done for you. You don't need to fight a battle that's already been won. You're forgiven. You're victorious. You're highly favored. Start trusting these things are true and stop trying to earn something that has already been freely given.

CHAPTER 7

2020 VISION

When I think of 20/20 vision, I think about clarity. Seeing with perfection. Nothing is blurred. Surrounded by beauty. The ability to see everything clearly. There's no hiding in clarity. There's no hiding from perfect vision. You can see every spot, wrinkle, or speck.

It's perfect sight.

That's how the year 2020 was supposed to start. It was the year promoted as "perfect vision, clarity, hope, destiny." Everything was going to be amazing in 2020. Unless you live under a rock, you know what I mean when I say 2020 started off pretty crazy and only got weirder with time.

For me, the first week of 2020 was painful. It was horrible. There was a moment I didn't know how to function, and I even felt like I didn't want to live.

We'll get to that in a moment.

The year 2020 started out with a bang. 3, 2, 1... Happy New Years! Fireworks, hugs, kisses. And then came a string of wildfires, airplane crashes in Iran and Pakistan, the death of basketball legend Kobe Bryant, social unrest over the killing of George Floyd, the deadly explosion in Beirut, and various natural disasters—many under the cloud of the coronavirus pandemic.

Everything shut down. People wearing masks. No one could leave their house. No church. No school. No amusement parks or movie theaters or restaurants. I can't even make this stuff up.

Perfect vision ended up being perfect destruction.

Depression rates skyrocketed all over the world. So did suicide rates. People were hurt and broken. Their hearts were heavy, and their minds were confused. When we're isolated in a home with the same few people twenty-four hours a day, seven days a week, things can get weird. Arguments, insecurities, "no toilet paper"! And that's only the beginning. People were losing their jobs, people were dying, and seemingly everything came to a stop.

I don't even have to say *imagine*. We all went through it. It's what we all have in common. And since you're reading this, you've survived the weirdest times of our lives. Maybe you've dealt with sadness, loneliness, depression, sadness, arguments, and hopelessness. What's happening with our marriages, children, churches, government. What is going to happen. Then, on top of all the pain and grief the pandemic caused, there was this new rule that was put into place: we have to wear *the mask*!

Now, if we rewind into the history of my life, I was born without a voice due to a growth in my airway that caused me to have issues breathing. These masks have made me struggle even more with my breathing and voice. I still haven't met one person who has said, "Oh my goodness, I just love wearing a mask. Don't you?" Whether it's because of anxiety, asthma, or a heart condition, many of us hate wearing the mask.

The year 2020 has not been perfect. But since you survived, congratulations! In 2020 your vision was definitely enhanced. You went through new challenges you never thought you could make it through, and the good news is you're still here. That's awesome. That tells me there's hope on the inside of you. Jesus has been the source to get you through. Even without community or church, you were able to survive.

As a pastor, I was scrambling to figure out how to get through the pandemic and how to operate without gathering. How can people still have a life-changing encounter with God online? And how can we inspire and move their souls with the understanding of Christ as their life? These questions were running through my head.

Doing everything through social media and Zoom created such a disconnect, and it forced us to try new ways to create connection with others. So coronavirus was of the devil. But God works it all out for our good. I wish I could say COVID-19 was the only battle I went through, but my 2020 had a dramatic start of its own.

One of my young brothers (AKA disciples) who I'm very close to called me on January 6 and let me know that his two-year-old son had fallen down the stairs and was now brain dead. He had been taken to the children's hospital a few hours from where I live. I spent a lot of time driving back and forth with other friends to pray for and support the family. We were believing for the best and praying for a miracle, hoping to see movement in his brain and body.

During one visit, I was playing my guitar and singing, worshipping the Lord at the feet of this boy's bed. His eyes began to twitch, and I started to sing louder and louder. Then his foot twitched and moved. Everyone looked around and said, "Do you see that?"

So we kept singing and thanking God for a miracle, knowing this boy would rise in Jesus's name. We continued to worship and pray. All of a sudden, the little boy lifted his hand in the air and then put it back down. We called the nurse and told her what happened—that he was responding to the music and worship.

She told us that sometimes the body will randomly move and do different things, so we shouldn't get too excited. Of course, we denied that and were believing his brain was responding.

Over the next few days, we continued praying for this boy and believing in what God could do. The doctors then told us to make final decisions and say our good-byes. His parents decided to donate his organs to five other children. And he went home to be with Jesus.

All I could do was cry and mourn. My world came crumbling down. I asked why God didn't heal this boy. Was my faith not enough? Was I doing something wrong? So many concerns flooded my mind as I questioned God's goodness and power. Why would something like this happen?

On the long drive home, I wept the whole time. My mind was so depleted. I was thinking of my three boys, ages three, four, and six years old. I wouldn't even know what to do if I lost one of my boys. How was it fair that someone could lose a child? My heart was hardened and my vision blurred. This was the beginning of another season of depression for me.

Depression is going from fullness of life to being a zombie. I was alive but not walking with life. I was a dead man walking. From clarity to blindness. From 2020 to complete blurriness. From perfect vision to complete darkness.

It reminds me of Saul before he became Paul. He was on his way to Damascus to persecute the Christians. He had natural sight, but then his eyes became scaled and he was blind for three days. He went from having vision to being blind. Seeing the light to walking in darkness.

I felt that way.

I was going into this new year with excitement, passion, and purpose, and was speaking hope and life and destiny to everyone around me. Then days into the new year, boom. Earthquake. Life shake. Devastation. I got knocked down. My vision was taken. My joy was stripped away. My hope was lost. I fell into complete sadness and depression.

With every other event and tragedy of the new year added, it was just destruction for me. I ended up doing the little boy's funeral and ministering to the family and encouraging everyone around me to get back up. It's so crazy because God can use us even in the moments when we feel useless and broken and defeated. Christ in us can help us be useful in moments of sorrow and grief to bring hope to others around us.

So there I was, being used by God and bringing positivity in the midst of this crazy year. Everyone was doing their best to balance things and figure life out. And just when it seemed like things were starting to go back to normal, I got a phone call at the end of May—from the same family!

"Will, can you get to the hospital now? Baby Jacob is not responding."

Just a bit of backstory on baby Jacob. He's the younger brother to the boy who passed away in January 2020. There's no other person I'm closer to than his father. I was at the gender reveal. I was at the baby shower. I was there when Jacob was born. I was the first one to hold him after his parents. I dedicated this baby to the Lord on the stage of our church. And now I was being told he was unresponsive. Are you kidding me? This family had been through enough.

I rushed to the hospital, and of course no one could get in because of COVID-19. But I was able to convince the nurses to let me in because I was Jacob's pastor and they considered me his uncle. I got in and stood at the foot of the bed and watched as seven doctors and nurses tried to bring him back to life.

Ten minutes passed. Nothing. Twenty minutes. Nothing. Needles in his legs, fists pumping on his little eight-month-old chest. They were doing everything they could. And nothing.

He was pronounced dead.

My heart was crushed. I was doing everything I could to comfort the family and be there for them, but on the inside I was devastated. I was crying as I was holding the family.

These are the moments when you think, *Can life get any crazier than this? What's the purpose of all of this? What is happening? Lord God, why? Someone needs to help explain these things!*

Full of sorrow and pain, I went home and hugged my sons once again. I cried so much and was trying to figure out how this could be true. For three days after that death, I had no emotions or words. My thoughts were very short.

Then I stumbled onto Psalm 55:22, which says to "cast your burdens on the Lord and He will sustain you and He will never permit the righteous to be moved." And there I was saying, "God, sustain me, strengthen me, help me, give me the heart to move forward. You say you will never permit the righteous to be moved and I am the righteous. I am your child."

Within moments, peace came over my mind and Philippians 1:6 came to my heart, reminding me that God is going to carry out the work He has started in me. It's not over! It may seem like death is around me, but I have the life of Christ in me, and He wants to be life to those around me.

As I talked to the father who lost these two boys, I was

doing everything I could to encourage him, yet he ended up flipping the script and encouraging me. He told me that he knew what his mission and call was—to speak hope and healing to those who are hurting, broken, and have lost children. He said he may have lost his children on earth but one day he'll see them again in heaven, and that as painful as it is, he knows God is going to get him through it all.

I was like, *What the heck! How are you preaching to me? How are you so strong and confident in God?* In that moment, God reminded me that He would fight for me and all I needed to do was be still (see Exodus 14:14).

Be still and know that He is God (see Psalm 46:10). He is going to get you through. Trust in Him. Keep walking. Speak to those mountains. Speak to those situations and problems and tell them to move because there's nothing impossible with God. It may seem like you've reached the end and there's no hope, but God *is* your hope. God will get you through this. It's not over. Your greatest days are ahead of you, and everything that has been lost in this world is just a moment. You have eternal life with Christ.

On November 14, right before midnight, my mom called me. My dad, who works construction on the freeway, was hit and run over. We didn't know much. We didn't know if my dad was even going to make it. Anxiety, worry, and concern are flooding me. Eight long hours go by until we heard from the hospital. My dad underwent numerous surgeries and was in recovery from a broken back, broken chest, broken ribs, broken knees, broken shins, broken ankles and feet, and that his recovery time would be a year before he would be able to walk.

My dad is also a pastor in Los Angeles. There were so many unanswered questions: *When would he get out? Who would preach for him? Who would take care of him? What does life look like for my parents now?*

My dad got released early in December. But the road ahead is still uncertain and his recovery is still a long journey ahead. We decided later that month that I would take over his church. Within weeks, the church has started growing and people are being saved. And my dad's story is moving and encouraging people because he survived and is giving people hope.

So what looked like something bad, God turned it around and worked it for my good and my dad's and is using this uncertain situation for the good of those around us.

Second Thessalonians 3:3 promises us this: "The Lord is faithful. He will establish you and guard you against the evil one." We know that Jesus is with us in every moment. God is faithful to never leave us (see Hebrews 13:5; 1 Corinthians 1:9). God cannot lie (see Numbers 23:19). So if he says it, we can believe it.

We have to decide to lay everything down and live in the hope that Christ has us covered. We need to open our eyes and see the goodness of God and see that He is wanting to use us to change lives and bring hope to those around us. I know it's easier to lie around, be negative, not see the good, and throw in the towel, but God has something greater for you.

Open your heart and talk to someone. Share your thoughts. Don't try to face these trials alone, especially if you've gone through some sort of loss, grief, or abandonment. Surround yourself with people and get locked into God's Word about you. Maybe your vision for 2020 was nothing close to what you've experienced, but don't go into these new seasons of your life with last year's mindset.

Every day is a new opportunity. Every day is a blessing.

Don't get to 2040 and say, "Man, I'm still struggling with what happened a few years back. My eyes will never be able to un-see all of that mess. I can't live in freedom." Maybe you might not be able to un-see what you've been through, but don't get so focused on what happened yesterday that you can't see the blessings of tomorrow.

Fix your eyes on Jesus.

Let's start getting clarity for the future. Perfect vision. Your greatest days are ahead.

CHAPTER 8

THE NEW MIND

Your season doesn't change your value. Nothing can change your worth. I love to paint pictures for people with my words, but right now I actually want to talk about a painted picture, the *Mona Lisa*.

There is so much value in the *Mona Lisa*. I tried to research the worth of the painting, and it is infinite; there's no number that can truly amount to its worth. It sits in a perfectly secure place in a museum. But if you were to take that same infinite-valued *Mona Lisa* painting out of the museum and place it in a broken-down shack in the middle of nowhere, that wouldn't change the value. Whether it's in the museum or in a shack, its value stays the same.

That's also you! You are God's masterpiece (see Ephesians 2:10). You might go through difficult trials in life or situations you can't fathom or explain, but it doesn't change your worth or value in God's eyes. The sacrifice has already been made. Jesus has already died the death. Your value is in place, and it cannot be stripped away from you or changed by what you do.

You may go through the difficult seasons. One day life

seems so amazing and great. You feel like you're in the museum of glory and everyone is looking at you in amazement, celebrating you and loving your life. Other days you feel like you're in the shack, all alone with no one seeing you. You feel like you don't matter. But even in that moment your value remains. You are precious. You are called. You are anointed for great things. You are royalty. You carry infinite value.

Romans 12:2 tells us to renew our mind and not conform to the pattern of this world. It's such an important thing for us to do as believers. To renew is to make brand new—to restore—and that's what God wants to do for us. He wants to restore our minds to newness and wholeness. That's one of the opportunities He gives us as His children. He won't force the process, though; it's up to us to change our mind. That's what He wants to do for you and me each day.

There are days when I feel glorious and excited about life. On other days I want to be like Adam Sandler in the movie *Click* and fast-forward through all my worries and pain. Renewing the mind is a process. I wish it was a one-time deal, but the reality is it's a daily fight of creating healthy habits to transform our mind.

Romans 12:2 finishes by saying we'll be able to test and approve God's will—His good, pleasing, and perfect will. What if told you that the will of God is always good for your life. He doesn't want bad things for you. You may hear my stories and think, *Wow, God put that on your shoulders. God made you go through all those trials and tribulations. Wow, brother, you're like Jonah and God sent you a whale to swallow you up. You must have been disobedient or God really, really wanted your attention!*

God doesn't desire bad things for his children. He doesn't cause bad things for us. And if you think God desired bad things for Jonah, you're wrong. If God hated Jonah so much, he would have sent a shark, not a whale. God is all about protection, guidance, and love for us. God is love. That's who He is. That's the best definition for Him.

God's will is revealed to us only by the renewing of our mind. If our minds are not renewed, we will think God hates us or doesn't care for us or He doesn't want anything to do with us or that He wants to destroy our life. God is not a boy with a magnifying glass on an anthill killing us.

God wants to use us, not destroy us. He wants to grow us and lead us into hope and understanding of our great position as His children. That's why renewing the mind is so important. It's how we can understand God's character and love for us. It allows us to see things through the finished work of Christ. It's the mind that God wants us to have, fully restored and fully open to see that Jesus lived a perfect and holy life on our behalf. That He died the sinner's death and rose again for us and ascended to heaven. That He did it for us and He did it as us. Now He's living in us and wants to live through us.

Renew your mind and know that you have purpose. Renew your mind and know that you are loved. Renew your mind and know that you are a child of God. Renew your mind and know that you are not your mistakes. Renew your mind and know that you are not identified by your past. Renew your mind and know that you are a new creation in Christ Jesus.

Live in confidence, knowing that everything Jesus did was for you. You are valuable. The *Mona Lisa* can't even compare to your worth. Walk restored and renewed. You have infinite worth and an amazing purpose.

I didn't always believe that I had true purpose. I believed the lies that I wasn't good enough. That depression will always be a part of me. That I was weak and just a broken, depressed, unfixable person. That I was useless, unlovable, and had no hope. But God says the opposite of that. God says we have a future and a hope. God says we have a destiny in Christ. And while we can sit and lie to ourselves that there's no hope for us —that there's no one that cares for us—God says we may be struck down but we won't be destroyed (2 Corinthians 4:9). We might go through the storm, but we'll make it to the other side.

There are struggles and difficulties in life and there will be moments when we think our life doesn't matter, but God says, "Your life is everything to me, and I sent my Son to restore you back to wholeness. You're not alone. You don't need to isolate yourself anymore. You don't have to dwell on your worst moments or the lies of the Enemy."

John 10:10 tells us that the Enemy comes to steal, kill, and destroy. He is trying to steal your peace, steal your joy, destroy your mind, and kill your destiny. He's trying to kill you. That's where suicide comes from—the lies of Satan. But Christ says He came to give us abundant life. You are worth everything that God paid. You are worth the life of Christ. And when you feel like there is no hope and no future, remember that you have a hope and a future in Christ Jesus.

Depression does not get the final word in your life. Christ does. Anxiety doesn't get the final word. Christ does. Pain doesn't get the last word. Jesus took the pain on your behalf, and He gets the final word. We have to stomp on these lies. We have to kill the Enemy's plan for us. We can no longer stand by and watch the Enemy rob us of our joy. We can't allow him to distract us from our future.

I used to think there was no hope—that I would never be able to come out of these ways of negative thinking. I remember getting on the phone and calling therapists and counselors and trying to figure out who could help me. I'm so glad that I did. We need to use the tools and people that God has trained and placed there to help us.

Sometimes Christians place a stigma on seeing a therapist

or counselor. Like if you go to see someone to share all your problems instead of going to Jesus only, you're not living in faith or in the will of God. Let me tell you this: Going to a counselor has been one of the most freeing things for me because I get to share everything with them and they're always going to give me practical advice and direction that I probably wouldn't have seen on my own.

If you don't have that, find a Christian therapist or counselor who will hear you out and speak hope into your life and situation. You need someone outside your normal circle of people to encourage you with God's Word and practical guidance.

God wants your mind restored, renewed, and back to fullness. He wants to get you to that place where your focus is on Him. There're also some natural things we can do. We all need to try something new. We can change our diet or daily habits. Having a healthy balance is essential to our energy and health. Or maybe it's more exercise, like walking around and getting outside. Anything can help. Get out in the sun, drink water, and get plenty of sleep.

Sleep is a hard one for me personally. My mind is always racing. But there are healthy things we can all do that can help us walk through seasons of difficulty and pain. Try to plan fun things to do with your friends and get involved with the community. And of course, seek professional help. Reach out. Don't get me wrong, you can have all these ideas and new patterns, but the real transformation is renewing your mind to the truth of Christ. Because if you don't have a renewed mind, then you can get all the sleep and exercise and have the best diet and still be depressed.

If you don't realize all that Christ has done for you, you'll never understand your value. You're more than enough to God. He paid Jesus for you. That's how valuable you are to Him.

You are worth the life of God's Son. You are more than enough. Speak that over yourself right now: "I am valuable. I am worthy. I am precious to God. I am enough." Fix your mind on those truths right now.

Fix your mind on Jesus. Renew your mind. Think God-thoughts toward yourself. That's what it means to have the mind of Christ. Do you realize that you have the mind of Christ? First Corinthians 2:16 says, "We have the mind of Christ." This doesn't mean we have all knowledge, but it does mean that we can think the thoughts God has toward us. We can choose to set our mind on His truth and His unfailing love and opinion of us.

I struggle with doing this. We all do. But Scripture also says that we can take every thought captive (see 2 Corinthians 10:5). And since Christ is in us, by His power we can choose to entertain thoughts or give them to Christ. We can choose to dwell on the past or dwell on the cross.

Haven't you noticed that when you focus on your past and your situation and your bad circumstances, you often lose sight of God's love and care for you? But when your eyes are on the cross and on Jesus, you have confidence that God is holding you and loving you. We have to remember who we are.

Our surroundings might change, but our value stays the same. Your value is infinite.

You are God's masterpiece.

CHAPTER 9

THE ABUNDANT LIFE

The life of much and plenty. The life that is full of joy, peace, happiness, grace, hope, and Jesus. A lot of us are living a life that is full of the absolute opposite of what I just listed. Maybe you're like me and can spend days in death. Full of sadness and depression. Maybe some sorrow, doubt, and confusion. That isn't what God wants for me or you.

Hear me though. This doesn't make me or you any less loved or valued or any less a child of God. My heart and mind are just fixed on everything else but Jesus. Think about it like going to a buffet. You walk through different sections—American food, Chinese food, fried foods, the vegan section, and everything in between—and choose what you fill your plate with.

The question is, what are you filling your life with? What are you filling your spiritual plate with? Are you taking on other people's worries and cares? Or the weight of someone's frustrations or marriage issues? Or your kids' or spouses' problems or social media battles? Or are you saying, "That doesn't belong on my plate"?

No one goes to a buffet and gets stuff they don't like. That's the awesome thing about free will and being able to choose what we want. Are you taking on identities like anxiety and depression and sorrow and pain instead of what God says about you in Christ?

In my case, I was putting things on my plate at an earlier age. As a young boy, I was in the court room watching my parents being convicted of things of their past. I was sitting there as the judge threw down his gavel and sentenced my parents to prison. The woman next to me, who I'd never met until that day, said, "You're going to come home with me."

I immediately started screaming and crying. Because of my hoarse voice, I'm sure I sounded like I was being tortured. I immediately ran down the aisle and begged for the judge to let my parents go.

It's crazy how situations can put us in moments of desperation. We long for and desire a different outcome. We all wish that some things could change. Many of us are in seasons we don't want to be in, whether that has to do with our nation or things that are required of us or what's happening in our home or at our job. We sometimes wish for a different outcome. And when we're desperate for something, sometimes we'll do anything to change our situation.

I think about the woman with the issue with blood who was desperate for a miracle (Luke 8:43–48). She had spent everything she had trying to get better, but she only got worse. Maybe you've been there. You've done everything in your own strength to see a different outcome. You're all out of sources with nothing left to give, and you find yourself desperately searching for hope and praying for a different outcome. And maybe you might just have to crawl through the crowd, raise your voice, or reach out in new ways.

The Bible says the woman reached out for Jesus's garment

—the very bottom of it. And when she did that, she received her miracle. I remember as I ran down the aisle, I threw myself over the dividers and rushed to my mom and hugged her leg tightly, begging for them to release her. The judge and the sheriff talked, and they agreed to release my mom.

Eyes were staring at us. Eyes of contempt looking down on my mom. If we go back to the story with the woman with the issue of blood, she touched the hem of the garment and was made whole. Before this encounter, she was restricted by people and wasn't allowed to leave her home. In those times, people with such a condition were considered contagious, which is why they were excluded.

This woman was trembling because Jesus asked, "Who touched me?" She spoke up and told Jesus it was her who touched Him and had been made whole. While everyone else was upset and looking down on her with eyes of contempt, Jesus didn't. While everyone else knew her as the woman with the issue, Jesus didn't see the issue. He didn't see her as a woman with a problem. Instead, He called her *daughter*. He saw beauty. He saw perfection. He saw hope. And He called out destiny. He doesn't see us as people with a problem either; He sees us as his children. He's not defining us by our past, but by what He has done.

No matter what we've done, He always welcomes us. He's not looking at us like those who looked at my mom with contempt. We are deeply loved by God, no matter what. He will never send us away. He won't allow us to be ensnared by the Enemy. You're His child and He loves you completely and without end.

God calls us to a place of knowing how loved we are and how much He cares for us and how He sees us for who we are and not what we've done. He sees us through the finished work and what Christ has accomplished and not through what we have or haven't accomplished or mistakes we've made. He sees us as beautiful, holy, righteous sons and daughters. And the great thing about being his sons and daughters is we can't be taken from His hands.

Isaiah 41:10 says we don't have to fear or be dismayed, because God is protecting us and holding us with His righteous right hand. The great thing about His right hand is He holds power there. He is protecting us and caring for us, and He won't allow anything to take us. As we understand who we are in Christ, we can live the abundant life God has promised.

The abundant life is not based on our works or our good deeds or how well we perform. It's not based on our perfection, but His perfection. It's not based on our thoughts, but His thoughts toward us. It's not based on our greatness, but how great He is. It's not based on our goodness, but His goodness that leads us to the abundant life.

So let's get our focus renewed and understand that God is good. That He loves us completely. That He has a purpose and destiny for us. That He will never neglect us or leave us. That He took the punishment. That the work is finished. You can walk in confidence and the abundant life that God has given you.

Stop believing the lies and live in the reality of the truth that there's nothing more you need to do but rest in who He is and what He's done. Don't put anything on your plate that doesn't need to be there. God only gives you what you need. Don't strive, trying to get answers to the things of this world. Reach out to Jesus and know that His answer is yes and amen. That He is not withholding anything from you and that He only wants the best for you. He sees you as His child.

In your moments of desperation, heartache, and pain, fall into the arms of Christ instead of falling into depression. That's easier said than done, but it will be more rewarding than anything you've ever experienced.

My prayer is that you would walk in confidence, knowing who you are as a child of God with your eyes fixed on the finished work of Jesus. Having no doubts of your position in Him. And being fully aware of your purpose and value.

Speak hope over yourself and live with confidence. Keep your eyes on Jesus and you will live with true freedom.

ABOUT WILL

Will Gutierrez is happily married to Amanda Gutierrez. He is the father to three boys - Ezra, Zion, and Zaiden. He is the lead pastor in Bakersfield and Los Angeles California. Will is a musician and a speaker and loves traveling around the country sharing the gospel. Connect personally with Will through social media:

 facebook.com/willspeakstruth
instagram.com/willspeaks

Made in the USA
Las Vegas, NV
31 December 2020